DATE DUE

APR 2 3 2012			
JUN 2 5 2012			
AUG 2 4 2012			
OCT 1 2012			
NOV 1 5 2014			

Demco, Inc. 38-293

The **STRANGEST** Plants on Earth

POISONOUS PLANTS

Margee Gould

PowerKiDS
press
New York

Published in 2012 by The Rosen Publishing Group, Inc.
29 East 21st Street, New York, NY 10010

First Edition

Editor: Jennifer Way
Book Design: Ashley Drago

Photo Credits: Cover, pp. 4, 5 (left, right), 19 (left, right) Shutterstock.com; pp. 6, 9 iStockphoto/ Thinkstock; p. 7 Oswald Eckstein/Getty Images; p. 8 Brian Gordon Green/Getty Images; p. 10 © www.iStockphoto.com/Mientje van den Boom; p. 11 © www.iStockphoto.com/inspireme; p. 12 © www.iStockphoto.com/Doug Cannell; p. 13 Bill Beatty/Getty Images; pp. 14–15 © www.iStockphoto.com/step2626; pp. 16–17 John Sohlden/Getty Images; p. 18 Bob Gibbons/ Getty Images; p. 20 © www.iStockphoto.com/Nico Smit; p. 21 DEA/D. Dagli Orti/De Agostini/ Getty Images.

Library of Congress Cataloging-in-Publication Data

Gould, Margee.
  Poisonous plants / by Margee Gould. — 1st ed.
      p. cm. — (The strangest plants on Earth)
  Includes index.
  ISBN 978-1-4488-4989-5 (library binding)
  1. Poisonous plants—Juvenile literature. I. Title. II. Series: Strangest plants on Earth
QK100.A1G68 2012
  581.6'59—dc22
                                    2010050512

Manufactured in the United States of America

CPSIA Compliance Information: Batch #WS11PK: For Further Information contact Rosen Publishing, New York, New York at 1-800-237-9932

Contents

Helpful or Deadly?

Plants are all around us. We count on many kinds of plants for food. We use the wood from trees to build things. Plants even help make the air we breathe. Most plants are helpful to us. There are some plants that do not help us, though. These plants are **poisonous**. They can make us sick or even kill us!

You might be wondering how a plant could kill someone. Some plants have **toxins** in their roots, leaves, or berries. If people or animals eat these plants, they can become sick. They can even die. Let's find out more about poisonous plants.

Above: This is the ripe berry of the bittersweet nightshade plant. Unripe berries of this plant are much more poisonous to people than ripe berries.

Right: The flower of bittersweet nightshade is purple. Bittersweet nightshade is native to Europe but is now found in woods all over North America.

It's Alive!

All plants need certain things to live. They need **carbon dioxide** from the air, as well as water and sunlight. They use these things to make their own food. Many plants use part of the energy they get from their food to grow flowers or berries. These plant parts have seeds in them. These seeds might one day grow new plants.

Some plants count on animals, such as birds or insects, to help them grow new plants. However, plant-eating animals, such as insects or cows, might eat a plant before it has a chance to put out new seeds. Some plants have developed **defenses** against this over time. One kind of defense is poison.

Above: The seed case of jimson weed gives the plant its nickname of thorn apple. All parts of this plant are poisonous.

Don't Eat That!

There are many kinds of poisonous plants. Plants such as azaleas and rhododendrons are common backyard plants that are poisonous. Their poison keeps these plants safe from deer and other hungry animals. Geraniums produce a toxin that keeps them safe from bugs such as Japanese beetles. The toxin **paralyzes** the beetle, or makes it so it cannot move. It wears off, but the beetle will likely dine elsewhere!

Sometimes only part of a plant is poisonous. It could also be poisonous only at a certain time in its growth cycle. Potato leaves and stems can be toxic. The toxic compounds are generally not found in the tuber, the part that is eaten.

Above: Azaleas, shown here, are poisonous to animals such as horses, sheep, and goats.

Close to Home

Many poisonous plants are beautiful. People even grow them in their yards and homes. Daffodils are a common and beautiful springtime flower. However, their sap can cause rashes. Worse, they have a poison called lycorine in their bulbs and leaves. This poison can cause stomach illness, convulsions, and even death.

Oleander is a well-liked flowering shrub in many people's gardens around the world. Oleander is one of the deadliest garden plants on Earth. Its leaves, berries, flowers, and stems are all poisonous. Oleander's toxins hurt many systems of the body. These include the **nervous system**, the **cardiovascular system**, and the **digestive system**.

11

A Closer Look at Poison Ivy

Have you have ever gotten the itchy rash that can come from touching poison ivy? If so, you likely want to know how to avoid it in the future.

Though poison ivy leaves are not always the same shape or size, there are some common things among the plants. Poison ivy plants have groups of three leaves

Left: Poison ivy grows in the eastern United States, parts of Canada, and in the mountains of Mexico. It can be found in forests, at the edges of fields, and along roadsides.

on a woody stem. They may have smooth edges or points. All parts of the poison ivy plant have an **allergen** called urushiol oil in them. Poison ivy sometimes climbs buildings or trees. It can also grow as a shrub or stay close to the ground.

Above: Urushiol causes a very itchy, long-lasting rash in most people. Even dead plants can give a rash for up to five years!

A Closer Look at Poison Oak

Poison oak is closely related to poison ivy. It grows mainly in the western parts of North America, though. Like its eastern relative, this plant has urushiol in it. Its leaves also grow in groups of three. Poison oak's leaves are generally **lobed**, though. The leaves are also rounder than those on poison ivy plants. Just as does poison ivy, poison oak grows groups of small white flowers in the spring. It then grows white berries.

People seem to be one of the few animals hurt by urushiol. Some people get a mild rash. Other people have **reactions** so strong they need to be treated at a hospital.

Birds eat poison oak berries and many animals feed on the plant's leaves.

Poison sumac grows in swamps and bogs in the eastern and central parts of the United States and Canada.

A Closer Look at Poison Sumac

Poison sumac is related to poison ivy and poison oak. It has the most urushiol of the three plants, though. Thankfully, it is not as common as its relatives. It grows in wet, swampy soil.

Poison sumac has 7 to 13 large, smooth leaves on each stem. In the spring, groups of white flowers bloom. In the fall, it has bunches of white berries, called **drupes**. Poison sumac grows as a shrub or small tree.

There are many kinds of sumac that are not poisonous. Those sumacs grow on dry ground. The sumac with red berries commonly seen along roadsides is not poisonous.

A Closer Look at Deadly Nightshade

Just from its name, deadly nightshade sounds like a plant to stay away from. This plant has green leaves and purple, bell-shaped flowers. It also has berries that are black when ripe.

The deadly nightshade's sweet, juicy berries might look good enough to eat. They are not! Two berries can be all it takes to kill a child. Just 10 to 20 berries are enough to kill an adult. This plant is deadly indeed. Nightshade paralyzes nerve endings in blood vessels, the heart, the stomach, and intestines.

Below: Deadly nightshade flowers are bell shaped and a lighter purple than are the plant's berries.

Above: Eggplants belong to the same plant family as deadly nightshade. They are not poisonous, though.

A Closer Look at Water Hemlock

Cattle graze near a stream. They eat many plants, including one that has roots that look like small turnips or sweet potatoes. Soon the cows that have eaten this plant will have seizures. They may enter comas or die. These cows have eaten water hemlock. Water hemlock is also known as cowsbane because it takes the lives of so many cows. A bane is something that causes death or pain.

Water hemlock is one of the deadliest plants in the United States. People in the past sometimes picked water hemlock thinking it was a parsnip, which is an edible root vegetable. It takes just one or two bites of water hemlock to kill a person.

Above: Here is a close-up of the water hemlock's flowers.

1 Wearing long sleeves, long pants, and shoes can keep you from getting urushiol on your skin. These clothes must be washed after wearing to get rid of the urushiol on them.

2 If you think you have touched poison ivy, poison oak, or poison sumac, wash that area of skin immediately. This can help prevent getting a rash.

3 There is an old saying that can help you avoid poison oak and poison ivy. It goes, "Leaves of three, let it be; berries white, poisonous sight."

It's a Fact!

4 Apple seeds, cherry pits, and peach pits are toxic. You would have to eat a lot of apple seeds to be hurt by them, though.

5 One of deadly nightshade's main poisons is atropine, which causes pupils to dilate, or widen. Eye doctors use small amounts of this poison to dilate people's pupils!

6 Buttercups have a toxin in them that can badly hurt the digestive system.

Glossary

allergen (A-ler-jen) Something that causes a bad reaction.

carbon dioxide (KAR-bin dy-OK-syd) A gas that plants take in from the air and use to make food.

cardiovascular system (kahr-dee-oh-VAS-kyuh-lur SIS-tem) The system that is made up of the heart, blood, and blood vessels.

defenses (dih-FENTS-ez) Things living things do that help keep them safe.

digestive system (dy-JES-tiv SIS-tem) The parts of the body that break down food into energy.

drupes (DROOPS) Fleshy fruits with one seed inside them.

lobed (LOHBD) Curved or rounded and sticking out or down.

nervous system (NER-vus SIS-tem) The system of nerve fibers in people or animals.

paralyzes (PER-uh-lyz-ez) Takes away feeling or movement.

poisonous (POYZ-nus) Causing pain or death.

reactions (ree-AK-shunz) Actions caused by things that have happened.

toxins (TOK-sunz) Poisons made by a plant or an animal that hurt another plant or animal.

Index

Web Sites

Due to the changing nature of Internet links, PowerKids Press has developed an online list of Web sites related to the subject of this book. This site is updated regularly. Please use this link to access the list:
www.powerkidslinks.com/spe/poiplant/